EARTHFORMS

MOUNTAINS

By Martha London

Consultant: Beth Gambro
Reading Specialist, Yorkville, Illinois

Minneapolis, Minnesota

Teaching Tips

Before Reading

- Look at the cover of the book. Discuss the picture and the title.
- Ask readers to brainstorm a list of what they already know about mountains. What can they expect to see in the book?
- Go on a picture walk, looking through the pictures to discuss vocabulary and make predictions about the text.

During Reading

- Read for purpose. Encourage readers to think about characteristics of mountains.
- Ask readers to look for the details of the book. How are mountains made?
- If readers encounter an unknown word, ask them to look at the sounds in the word. Then, ask them to look at the rest of the page. Are there any clues to help them understand?

After Reading

- Encourage readers to pick a buddy and reread the book together.
- Ask readers to name two animals found on mountains. Find the pages that tell about these animals.
- Ask readers to write or draw something they learned about mountains.

Credits

Cover and title page, © hadynyah/iStock; 3, © hadynyah/iStock; 5, © hadynyah/iStock; 7, © milehightraveler/iStock; 8–9, © Ozant/Shutterstock; 11, © christiannafzger/iStock; 12, © Veniamin/Adobe Stock; 13, © Alberto Masnovo/iStock; 14–15, © NathalieNasrallah/iStock; 17, © PhotoMet/Shutterstock; 18, © Wirestock/iStock; 19, © bgsmith/iStock; 20–21, © WLDavies/iStock; 22T, © pingebat/Shutterstock; 22M, © Jamling Tenzing Norgay/Wikimedia Commons; 22B, © maroznc/iStock; 23TL, © molchanovdmitry/iStock; 23TM, © Vershinin-M/iStock; 23TR, © hadynyah/iStock; 23BL, © christiannafzger/iStock; 23BM, © maroznc/iStock; 23BR, © 1365551519/iStock.

See BearportPublishing.com for our statement on Generative AI Usage.

Library of Congress Cataloging-in-Publication Data

Names: London, Martha, author.
Title: Mountains / by Martha London.
Description: Minneapolis, MN : Bearport Publishing Company, 2025. | Series: Earthforms | Includes bibliographical references and index.
Identifiers: LCCN 2024023191 (print) | LCCN 2024023192 (ebook) | ISBN 9798892326247 (library binding) | ISBN 9798892327046 (paperback) | ISBN 9798892326643 (ebook)
Subjects: LCSH: Mountains--Juvenile literature.
Classification: LCC GB512 .L66 2025 (print) | LCC GB512 (ebook) | DDC 551.43/2--dc23/eng/20240606
LC record available at https://lccn.loc.gov/2024023191
LC ebook record available at https://lccn.loc.gov/2024023192

Copyright © 2025 Bearport Publishing Company. All rights reserved. No part of this publication may be reproduced in whole or in part, stored in any retrieval system, or transmitted in any form or by any means, electronic, mechanical, photocopying, recording, or otherwise, without written permission from the publisher.

For more information, write to Bearport Publishing, 5357 Penn Avenue South, Minneapolis, MN 55419.

Contents

Tall and Rocky.................. 4

Mount Everest 22

Glossary 23

Index 24

Read More 24

Learn More Online......................... 24

About the Author 24

Tall and Rocky

It is cold on the mountain.

White snow covers the **peak** at the top.

The wind blows all around.

Brr!

Mountains are big piles of dirt and rock.

They are so tall you can see them from far away.

There are mountains all around the world.

How do mountains form?

Earth's ground is made of big pieces of rock.

Sometimes, two pieces smash together.

Rocks push up and turn into mountains.

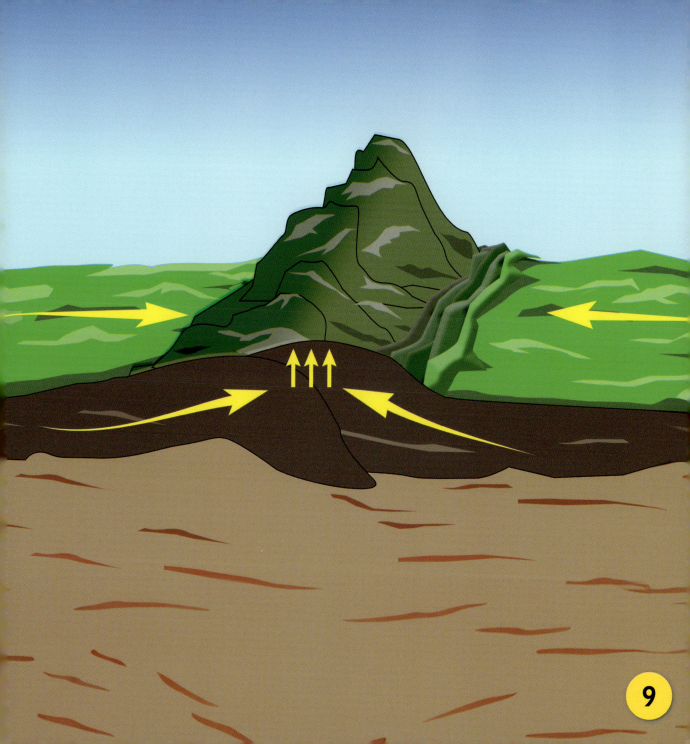

Most mountains form in a **range**.

A range is a line of mountains.

These ranges can be very long.

Volcanoes are mountains that stand on their own.

Hot melted rock called **lava** pushes out of the ground.

It piles up and cools to make a volcano.

Lava

Mountains are always changing.

Wind and rain break off tiny pieces of rock.

This makes mountains smaller after many years.

Weather changes from a mountain's bottom to its peak.

At the bottom, there may be lots of rain.

Mountain peaks are colder and may get snow.

Many plants and animals live on mountains.

Foxes play in tall grass at the bottom.

Sheep climb on rocks near the peak.

Some people **hike** on mountains.

Others climb up with ropes.

They look at the view from the top.

Mountains are amazing!

Mount Everest

Mount Everest has the highest peak above the sea!

Mount Everest is part of a mountain range in Asia.

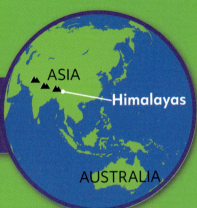

Mountain climbers first reached the top of Everest in 1953.

Mount Everest is **sacred** to many people from the area.

Glossary

hike to go on a long walk, often uphill

lava melted rock coming from a volcano

peak the highest point on a mountain

range a series of things in a line

sacred very important and respected

volcanoes mountains or cracks in Earth's crust from which melted rock comes out

Index

animals 18
lava 12,
peak 4, 16, 18, 22
snow 4, 16
volcano 12
weather 16
range 10, 22

Read More

Gibbons, Gail. *Volcanoes (Explore the World with Gail Gibbons).* New York: Holiday House, 2021.

Neuenfeldt, Elizabeth. *Mountain Animals (What Animal Am I?).* Minneapolis: Bellwether Media, 2023.

Learn More Online

1. Go to **FactSurfer.com** or scan the QR code below.
2. Enter "**Earthforms Mountains**" into the search box.
3. Click on the cover of this book to see a list of websites.

About the Author

Martha London lives in Minnesota. She loves spending time outside.